PUNCH BOWLS
and pitcher drinks

PUNCH BOWLS
and pitcher drinks

recipes for delicious big-batch cocktails

Clarkson Potter/Publishers
NEW YORK

Published in the United States by Clarkson
Potter/Publishers, an imprint of the Crown
Publishing Group, a division of Random
House LLC, a Penguin Random House
Company, New York.
www.crownpublishing.com
www.clarksonpotter.com

CLARKSON POTTER is a trademark and
POTTER with colophon is a registered trademark
of Random House LLC.

Library of Congress Cataloging-in-
Publication Data
Punch bowls and pitcher drinks: recipes for
delicious big-batch cocktails / Recipes by Jeanne
Kelley and Sarah Tenaglia; photographs by
Andrea Bricco. — First edition.
    Includes index.
    1. Punches (Beverages).   I. Kelley,
Jeanne, author.   II. Tenaglia, Sarah, author.
III. Clarkson Potter (Firm).
    TX815.K42   2015
    641.87'4—dc23   2014010345

ISBN 978-0-8041-8644-5
eBook ISBN 978-0-8041-8643-8

Printed in China

Book and cover design by Stephanie Huntwork
Text by Jeanne Kelley and Sarah Tenaglia
Book and cover photographs by Andrea Bricco
Prop styling by Alicia Buszczak
Produced by CookIt Media

10 9 8 7 6 5 4 3 2 1

First Edition

CONTENTS

INTRODUCTION

AH, PUNCH! Has there ever been a concoction that brings so many people together? Standing by the punch bowl is always a safe bet, whether or not you consider yourself a wallflower—because who wouldn't want the opportunity to excuse himself or herself for a glass of delicious fruity, sparkling goodness? And though a punch isn't necessarily more enjoyable than a cocktail, we simply wouldn't have a single-serving drink without first having perfected big batches for a crowd: Punches are meant for gatherings, meant to be mixed and sipped and adjusted and mixed again, something you can blend and taste at your leisure. And punch is constantly open to reinvention, whether you're serving it up in a big pitcher stirred with a tall spoon or in a giant glass tureen over a beautiful ice mold. You can go classic, with a **Planter's Punch (page 41)**, or go fresh and foodie and muddle some herbs or spices into a batch of **Spiked Pineapple Agua Fresca with Sage and Serrano (page 66)**. There's no wrong way to enjoy these beverages, even in recipes where there's not a drop of alcohol.

Each recipe in this book can be adapted to whatever serving size you may need, though they are best enjoyed when served up for a group of six or more. (See A Few Notes About the Perfect Punch, opposite, for advice on how to get exactly the right amount of booziness in each batch of punch.) We also have suggestions for making colorful flower and fruit ice molds for each recipe, to keep your punch both adequately chilled and beautifully displayed over the course of your party. And many of the recipes here recommend specific glasses or serving methods for the punch in question—but those are just our recommendations, and you should feel free to mix and match serving styles to fit your party needs. Hoping to serve a batch of **Peachy Moonshine (page 74)** in tall glasses rather than mason jars? Sounds good! Want to hollow out some coconuts and use them to serve up the **Island Girl Punch (page 95)** with paper umbrellas? Go for it! There are a million ways to serve up these lovely drinks, so get creative . . .

In *Punch Bowls and Pitcher Drinks*, there are fifty irresistible recipes—all perfectly delectable and portable—and once you see how easy it is to dress up this classic beverage, you'll likely dream up variations of your own. The possibilities are endless. Just make sure to keep this book around for inspiration. Now go brew up a batch of something delicious!

A FEW NOTES ABOUT THE PERFECT PUNCH

Punch is a blend of liquids: mostly juice and spirits, and frequently brewed tea. Acid from citrus, potency of distilled beverages, and sweetness from syrup, sugar, liqueurs, mixers, and fruit are the key flavor variables in the bowl, and in order to get the best-tasting batch, you'll want to keep the following in mind.

Citrus juice from limes, lemons, oranges, tangerines, grapefruit, and kumquats has a star role in several of these recipes; note that the tartness of citrus varies considerably from backyard tree fruit to purchased fruit from the farmer's market or the grocery store. Hyper-fresh backyard citrus will have a more intense flavor. Always taste and adjust the punch while blending, as you may need to increase the amounts to get the desired balance of sweetness and acidity.

Unless the recipe specifies, you do not need to peel the citrus, fruit, or vegetables used in these punches. In many cases the peel or rind of a fruit adds a note of necessary bitterness to counter the sweeter meat of the fruit, and also helps infuse the punch with more aromatic flavors. To make a twist of citrus peel to float in these punches, slice a thin layer of peel off a ripe lemon, lime, or orange with a sharp knife. Cut the pith off the rind so you have one long piece of peel, then twist the peel into a curlicue shape to garnish each glass.

Brands of alcohol also vary considerably. In order to get the right balance, we recommend adding the amount of liquor called for in the recipes (the smaller amount if a range is listed). If, after tasting, you want a more potent mix, add more liquor by the tablespoonful to taste. Go with what suits your palate.

Some folks really prefer sweet drinks. If a recipe calls for a flavored syrup or sugar, a little more can be stirred into the mix, but start with the recommended amount.

Any of the recipes in this book can be served in a punch bowl. If serving a hot beverage, use a metal (not glass) punch bowl. If the punch has a whipped cream topping, serve the topping in a small bowl alongside.

Many of these punch recipes get "topped off" or finished with sparkling wine or water. Here too is an opportunity to personalize the drinks by adjusting the amount of bubbly liquid: Start with just a splash, and increase as desired.

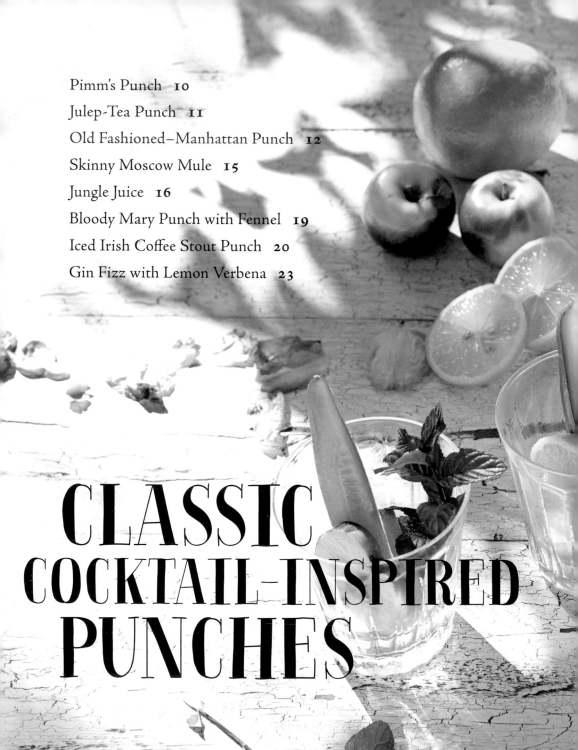

CLASSIC COCKTAIL–INSPIRED PUNCHES

PIMM'S PUNCH (PAGE 10)

PIMM'S
PUNCH

London oyster-bar owner James Pimm invented a gin-based drink in the 1840s, and it was bottled as Pimm's No. 1. Five additional Pimm's Cups were created with a variety of alcohols, all the way up to No. 6 (vodka-based), but Pimm's No. 1 is the only one available in the United States. This drink is still the official beverage at Wimbledon. Light and refreshing, it's perfect for a summer garden party. **SERVES 6 TO 8**

8 ½-inch-thick unpeeled cucumber rounds or
    spears (from 1 cucumber)
1 large orange, cut into rounds, seeds removed
1 large lemon, cut into rounds, seeds removed
1 large apple, cored and cut into wedges
16 fresh mint sprigs
2 cups Pimm's No. 1 Cup
½ cup fresh lemon juice
2½ cups chilled ginger ale or lemon-lime soda
1½ cups chilled sparkling water
Ice cubes

1 Combine the cucumber, fruits, and half the mint in a large pitcher. Using a muddler or a wooden spoon, press on the fruit and mint several times. Add the Pimm's and lemon juice. Refrigerate for 1 hour, then mix in the ginger ale and sparkling water.

2 Fill tumblers with ice cubes, then add the chilled punch and its fruits. Garnish with the remaining mint sprigs.

JULEP-TEA
PUNCH

This punch has all the bourbon flavor of the classic southern drink, but it's lightened with briskly flavored black tea. Serve this fun and less-potent adaptation in silver cups for a Kentucky Derby party. **SERVES 12**

3 Earl Grey tea bags
1½ cups bourbon whiskey
¾ cup Mint Simple Syrup (page 106)
Crushed ice
12 fresh mint sprigs

1 Bring 3 cups water to a boil in a medium saucepan. Add the tea bags and remove the saucepan from the heat. Cool completely. Discard the tea bags.

2 Pour the tea into a large pitcher; refrigerate until cold. Mix in the bourbon and mint syrup. Fill 12 cups or goblets with crushed ice. Place a mint sprig in each cup and pour the julep tea over the ice. Stir well, bruising the mint slightly, and serve.

OLD FASHIONED– MANHATTAN

PUNCH

Here is a sophisticated punch that combines elements of two favorite whiskey cocktails: an Old Fashioned and a Manhattan. Keep the punch cool with Cherry-Tangerine Ice Cubes (see below); you can find the oversize silicone ice cube molds at cookware stores or online. **SERVES 4**

8 tangerine or orange peel strips
3 tablespoons maraschino cherry juice
  (from a jar of maraschino cherries)
4 maraschino cherries
½ cup bourbon whiskey
½ cup sweet red vermouth
½ cup fresh tangerine or orange juice
½ cup brewed black tea, chilled
8 dashes of Angostura bitters
4 Cherry-Tangerine Ice Cubes (see below)

CHERRY-TANGERINE ICE CUBES

Place 1 maraschino cherry and 1 tangerine or orange slice in each of 4 oversize ice cube molds. Fill the molds with water and freeze until solid.

1 Combine the tangerine peel, cherry juice, and cherries in a 1-quart pitcher. Using a muddler or the handle of a wooden spoon, press on the fruits several times. Add the bourbon, vermouth, tangerine juice, tea, and bitters to the pitcher and stir to combine.

2 Divide the mixture among 4 short glasses. Add the ice cubes; stir to blend.

SKINNY MOSCOW
MULE

The Moscow Mule cocktail was invented in Los Angeles in the 1940s and was wildly popular in Hollywood. We follow tradition by serving this in copper mugs, but our version has been lightened up with green tea, diet ginger beer, and grated fresh ginger to make it the perfect fit for the health-conscious drinker. To make the garnish, cut long, thin slices of unpeeled gingerroot. **SERVES 4**

2 cups chilled diet ginger beer (such as Bundaberg)
    or ginger ale
1 cup vodka
1 cup brewed green tea, chilled
½ cup fresh lime juice
1 teaspoon grated peeled fresh ginger
1 teaspoon agave nectar, or more to taste (optional)
Ice cubes
4 lengthwise slices unpeeled fresh ginger,
    for garnish
8 thin lime slices, for garnish

1 Combine the ginger beer, vodka, tea, lime juice, and grated ginger in a 1½-quart pitcher. Sweeten to taste with the agave nectar, if desired.

2 Fill 4 copper mugs or tumblers with ice. Add the ginger beer mixture. Garnish with the fresh ginger slices and lime slices.

JUNGLE
JUICE

Popular in college (and every campus has its own variation), this potent punch, also known as College Punch, Hunch Punch, and Wopatui, combines several kinds of alcohol and fruit juices along with sliced fresh fruit. This version is not as potent as most, but because the fruit juice masks the taste of the alcohol, it's best to serve it in small cups. **SERVES 16**

1½ cups fresh orange juice
1½ cups fresh grapefruit juice
1½ cups apple juice
1½ cups pineapple juice
1½ cups white cranberry or white grape juice
1 cup vodka
1 cup light or gold rum
1 cup gin
1 cup tequila
½ cup fresh lemon juice
4 cups assorted fruit such as grapes, sliced apple, sliced or cubed pineapple, and sliced orange
Ice cubes

1 Mix the orange juice, grapefruit juice, apple juice, pineapple juice, cranberry juice, vodka, rum, gin, tequila, and lemon juice in a large bucket or punch bowl. Add the fruit and refrigerate until cold, about 2 hours.

2 Fill 16 small glasses with ice. Ladle the punch over the ice, including some fruit in each serving.

BLOODY MARY
PUNCH with fennel

A brunch classic updated with fennel and celery-olive ice cubes. For a large gathering, triple the recipe and serve in a punch bowl with an ice mold made with olives and celery leaves (see page 108). **SERVES 6**

3 cups chilled good-quality tomato juice

1⅓ cups vodka

½ cup fresh lemon juice

2 teaspoons hot pepper sauce

2 teaspoons Worcestershire sauce

1 teaspoon Smoky Fennel Salt (see below)

Freshly cracked black pepper, to taste

6 Celery-Olive Ice Cubes (see below) or regular ice cubes

6 fennel stalks, for garnish

6 celery stalks, for garnish

SMOKY FENNEL SALT

Crush 1 teaspoon kosher salt, 1 teaspoon fennel seeds, and ¼ teaspoon smoked paprika with a mortar and pestle.

CELERY-OLIVE ICE CUBES

Place celery leaves and pimiento olives in an ice cube tray. Fill the tray with water, and freeze overnight.

1 Stir the tomato juice, vodka, lemon juice, hot pepper sauce, Worcestershire sauce, fennel salt, and black pepper in a large pitcher.

2 Fill 6 glasses with celery-olive ice cubes. Pour the tomato juice mixture over the ice. Garnish with the fennel and celery stalks.

ICED IRISH COFFEE STOUT

PUNCH

Chocolate stout meets coffee and whiskey in this adult drink that's great year-round. **SERVES 4**

½ **cup chilled whipping cream**
½ **teaspoon sugar**
2 **cups chilled chocolate stout**
¼ **cup brewed strong coffee, chilled**
2 **tablespoons Irish whiskey**
2 **teaspoons crème de cacao**
4 **cups crushed ice**
Chocolate syrup, for garnish

1 Whisk the cream and sugar together in a large bowl until very loosely whipped. Cover and refrigerate until ready to use. Mix the stout, coffee, whiskey, and crème de cacao in a large pitcher.

2 Fill 4 small glasses with crushed ice. Pour the stout mixture over the ice. Top with the whipped cream. Drizzle with chocolate syrup and serve.

GIN
FIZZ with lemon verbena

Lemon verbena makes a beautiful and fragrant garnish.
You can find it at nursery stores and farmer's markets.

SERVES 4

¾ cup Lemon Verbena Simple Syrup
   (page 106), divided
¾ cup gin, divided
½ cup whipping cream, divided
4 large egg whites, divided
½ cup fresh lemon juice, divided
⅛ teaspoon orange-flower water
6 cups ice cubes, divided
Freshly grated nutmeg
Fresh lemon verbena sprigs (optional, for garnish)

NOTE

This recipe contains raw egg whites and should not be served to pregnant women, the elderly, or anyone with a compromised immune system.

1 Combine 6 tablespoons of the syrup, 6 tablespoons of the gin, ¼ cup of the cream, 2 of the egg whites, ¼ cup of the lemon juice, ¹⁄₁₆ teaspoon of the orange-flower water, and 3 cups of the ice in a blender. Blend until smooth and foamy. Pour the blended liquid into 2 wine glasses.

2 Repeat with the second batch of ingredients, and pour into 2 glasses.

3 Sprinkle the drinks with nutmeg and garnish with lemon verbena sprigs, if desired.

SANGRIAS
AND CHAMPAGNE-BASED
PUNCHES

STRAWBERRY-RHUBARB SANGRIA (PAGE 28)

STRAWBERRY-RHUBARB

SANGRIA

This light sangria is made with rosé and accented with fresh rhubarb syrup and sliced strawberries.

SERVES 4 TO 6

1 750-ml bottle dry rosé wine

1 cup Rhubarb Simple Syrup (page 107)

8 medium strawberries, hulled and sliced

1 stalk rhubarb, cut diagonally into 1-inch-thick slices

4 2-inch-long strips lemon peel

Ice cubes

1 Mix the wine, syrup, strawberries, rhubarb, and lemon peel in a large pitcher. Cover and refrigerate for 2 to 4 hours to allow the flavors to develop.

2 Fill 4 to 6 wine glasses or tumblers with ice. Pour the sangria and fruit over the ice and serve.

APPLE-THYME
SPARKLER

The fresh thyme is optional, but it does add a nice twist. Use the best apple juice you can find. Farmer's markets and upscale markets are usually good sources.

SERVES 4

2 cups chilled hard apple cider
1 cup chilled good-quality apple juice or apple cider
¼ cup Applejack (apple brandy)
Ice cubes
4 fresh thyme sprigs (optional, for garnish)
1 to 2 small apples, cored and thinly sliced,
   for garnish

Mix the hard cider, apple juice, and Applejack in a small pitcher. Fill 4 small punch cups or glasses with ice. Add 1 thyme sprig and 1 apple slice to each. Pour the punch over the ice and serve.

WHITE SANGRIA
EXOTIQUE

Exotic fruits impart heavenly flavor to this light punch. Liqueurs, such as St-Germain, an elderflower liqueur, and Domaine de Canton, a ginger liqueur, can be added for additional flower-and-spice sweetness. **SERVES 6**

1 750-ml bottle chilled Pinot Grigio
1 15-ounce can lychees in their syrup
½ cup light rum
½ cup fresh lemon juice
4 tangerines, each cut into 3 rounds
2 kiwis, peeled and sliced
1½ cups peeled and chopped pineapple
1 tablespoon St-Germain elderflower liqueur (optional)
1 tablespoon Domaine de Canton ginger liqueur (optional)
Ice cubes

1 Mix the wine, lychees and syrup, rum, lemon juice, tangerines, kiwis, pineapple, and liqueurs, if using, in a large pitcher. Refrigerate for 2 to 4 hours to allow the flavors to develop.

2 Fill 6 glasses with ice. Pour the sangria and fruit over the ice and serve.

RED WINE
SANGRI-LA

This simple sangria is easy to make and so delicious. Almost any fruit will work, so use whatever is in season.

SERVES 8

1 750-ml bottle chilled dry red wine
3 cups fresh orange juice
¾ cup Grand Marnier
½ cup brandy
1 crab apple, cored and sliced
1 Forelle pear, cored and sliced
1 orange, sliced, seeds removed
1 tangerine, peeled and sliced, seeds removed
1 basket fresh blackberries (about 1½ cups)
Ice cubes

1 Mix the wine, orange juice, Grand Marnier, brandy, crab apple slices, pear slices, orange slices, tangerine slices, and blackberries in large container. Refrigerate 2 to 4 hours to allow the flavors to develop.

2 Ladle the sangria with the fruit into a small punch bowl. Fill 8 wine glasses with ice. Ladle the sangria over the ice, including fruit in each portion, and serve.

BLACKBERRY KIR
PUNCH

Kir Royale (champagne and crème de cassis) is raised to a new level with muddled blackberries and lime wedges and a splash of elderflower liqueur. To serve in a punch bowl, add the muddled berries and lime, then mix in the liqueurs and fill with champagne. Add an ice mold made with berries and lime wedges (see Tips for Ice Molds, page 108). **SERVES 4**

8 fresh blackberries or 8 frozen blackberries, thawed

4 lime wedges, seeds removed

3 tablespoons crème de cassis

3 tablespoons St-Germain elderflower liqueur

8 ice cubes

1 750-ml bottle chilled brut champagne or sparkling wine

1 Place the berries and lime wedges in a large glass measuring cup. Using a muddler or the handle of a wooden spoon, press on the fruits several times. Mix in the crème de cassis and St-Germain.

2 Add 2 ice cubes to each of 4 large champagne flutes. Divide the berry-lime mixture among the flutes. Top off the glasses with champagne; stir gently to combine.

MEYER LEMON DROP CHAMPAGNE
PUNCH

You'll notice that this punch has no added sugar: It's not necessary when the limoncello is already so sweet, and the sugar rim gives a little extra crunch. Better to keep this drink on the slightly tart and tangy side instead of giving your guests a toothache. **SERVES 8**

1 cup fresh Meyer lemon juice
½ cup vodka
½ cup limoncello
1 cup chilled brut champagne or sparkling wine
2 cups ice cubes
8 Meyer Lemon Sugar–Rimmed Glasses
(see below)

MEYER LEMON SUGAR–RIMMED GLASSES

Use a fine-hole Microplane or other grater to remove the zest from 1 Meyer lemon. Mix the zest with ¼ cup sugar on a small plate, stirring to release the lemon oils. Rub 1 lemon wedge around the rim of small champagne coupes to moisten lightly. Dip the rims in the lemon sugar to coat.

1 Mix the Meyer lemon juice, vodka, and limoncello in a medium pitcher. Chill until cold, about 2 hours.

2 Add the champagne and ice to the lemon mixture and stir until icy cold. Strain into 8 sugar-rimmed glasses and serve.

GRAPE HARVEST CHAMPAGNE
PUNCH

Here's a way to celebrate the grape season, which in the United States runs from late July through early December. Let these beautiful red grapes swim in a big pool of champagne and sweet French Sauternes over clusters of grapes frozen into an ice mold (see Note below). **SERVES 16**

7 cups seedless red grapes

2 750-ml bottles chilled Sauternes

4 lemon peel twists (see page 7)

1 Grape Cluster Ice Mold (see below)

1 750-ml bottle chilled dry champagne or sparkling wine, or more to taste

Ice cubes (optional)

GRAPE CLUSTER ICE MOLD

Fill a mold with water to 2 inches from the top. Add clusters of red, green, or black grapes (some should protrude at the surface). Freeze overnight; the frozen mold can be kept up to 1 month, wrapped tightly in plastic. To release, turn the mold upside down under running water until the ice releases.

1 Working in batches, puree the grapes with the Sauternes in a blender. Strain into a large bowl, pressing on the solids to release as much liquid as possible; add the lemon twists.

2 Place the ice mold in a large punch bowl. Add the Sauternes mixture, then the bottle of champagne. Taste, adding more champagne if you like. Serve over ice cubes, if desired.

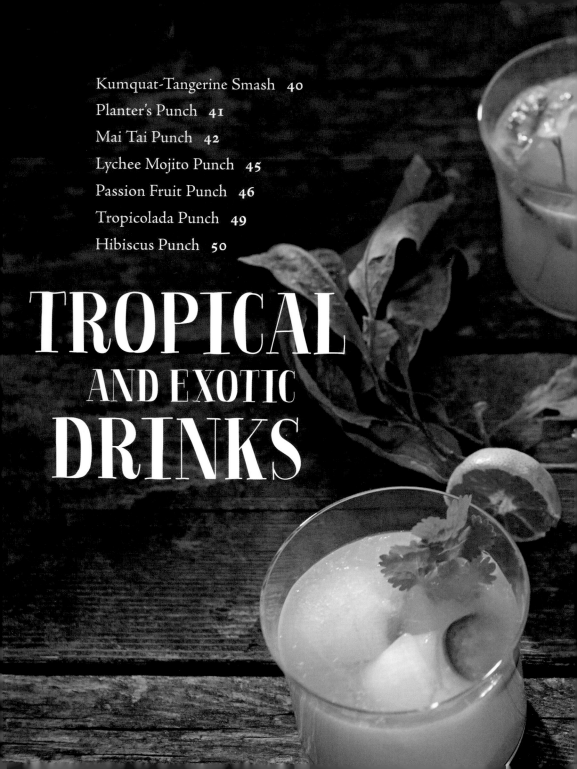

TROPICAL
AND EXOTIC
DRINKS

KUMQUAT-TANGERINE SMASH (PAGE 40)

KUMQUAT-TANGERINE
SMASH

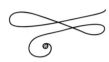

Jalapeño adds a subtle spicy kick and cilantro lends an herbal note. **SERVES 4**

12 kumquats, halved and seeded
8 fresh cilantro sprigs
¼ cup sugar
¾ cup silver tequila made with 100% agave
½ cup fresh tangerine juice
¼ cup fresh lime juice
2 slices jalapeño chile, seeded
1 cup chilled sparkling water
Ice cubes

1 Using a muddler or the handle of a wooden spoon, muddle the kumquats, cilantro, and sugar in a medium bowl until the kumquats break apart. Add the tequila, tangerine juice, lime juice, and jalapeño. Stir to dissolve the sugar. Mix in the sparkling water.

2 Transfer the punch to a small pitcher. Fill 4 small glasses with ice. Pour the kumquat punch over the ice. Stir to blend.

PLANTER'S
PUNCH

Planter's punch is an old-school classic. Here the strong mix is freshened up with lively pomegranate juice instead of red-dye grenadine. **SERVES 6**

1½ cups 100% pomegranate juice (such as Pom)
1½ cups gold rum
¾ cup fresh lime juice
¾ cup Lime Simple Syrup (page 107)
1½ teaspoons Angostura or other bitters
Crushed ice

1 Stir the pomegranate juice, rum, lime juice, lime syrup, and bitters together in a small pitcher. Refrigerate until cold, about 2 hours.

2 Pack 6 glasses with crushed ice. Pour the punch over the ice and serve.

MAI TAI
PUNCH

Mai tai means "out of this world" in Tahitian. The original drink was invented in 1944 by Victor Bergeron, owner of the Polynesian-themed Trader Vic's restaurant chain in Oakland, California. There are dozens of recipes for mai tais, but this one uses an allspice simple syrup for a distinctive flavor. Make an ice mold with sliced oranges, limes, and pineapple and fresh mint. This recipe uses a rum "floater," an old-school cocktail term for a half shot (or tablespoonful) of booze added to the top of a mixed drink. Because the liquor has a higher proof than the drink, it floats. **SERVES 4**

1 cup chilled fresh orange juice
1 cup gold rum
½ cup chilled pineapple juice
½ cup fresh lime juice, or more to taste
¼ cup Amaretto liqueur
⅓ cup Allspice Simple Syrup (page 107)
Crushed ice
4 tablespoons dark rum (optional)
4 fresh mint sprigs, for garnish
4 maraschino cherries, for garnish

1 Mix the orange juice, rum, pineapple juice, lime juice, Amaretto, and allspice syrup in a small pitcher. Taste, adding more lime juice, if desired.

2 Fill 4 short glasses or tumblers with crushed ice. Add the punch and top with a dark rum floater, if desired. Garnish with mint sprigs and cherries.

LYCHEE MOJITO
PUNCH

Lychee fruit lends a tropical note to the classic Cuban rum cocktail of muddled mint, sugar, and lime juice.

SERVES 4

8 whole canned sweetened lychees, plus 1 cup of
 their syrup
24 fresh mint leaves
8 lime slices (from about 2 limes), seeds removed
3 tablespoons fresh lime juice, or more to taste
¾ cup white rum
½ cup chilled sparkling water
Ice cubes
4 fresh mint sprigs, for garnish

1 Combine the whole lychees, mint leaves, lime slices, and the 3 tablespoons of lime juice in the bottom of a small pitcher. Using a muddler or the handle of a wooden spoon, press gently on the solids to lightly crush. Mix in the lychee syrup, rum, and sparkling water. Taste, adding more lime juice if desired.

2 Fill 4 tall glasses with ice. Add the punch and some fruit to each glass. Garnish with mint sprigs and serve.

PASSION FRUIT
PUNCH

A great choice for a tropical party. Frozen passion fruit pulp can be found at some specialty foods stores and supermarkets. Nonpoisonous purple orchids can be found at most florists. SERVES 16

3 cups gold rum

2 cups frozen unsweetened passion fruit pulp (such as Goya)

½ cup fresh lime juice, or more to taste

2 tablespoons Cointreau

4½ × 2-inch lime peel strips

4 cups chilled mandarin orange soda

Orchid and Lime Ice Mold (see below)

Ice cubes

Nonpoisonous purple orchids (optional, for garnish; see page 108)

ORCHID AND LIME ICE MOLD

Fill a 2-quart mold with water to 2 inches from the top. Add a few orchids, sliced limes, and halved passion fruit, if available (the fruit and leaves will float). Freeze overnight or wrap the frozen mold tightly in plastic wrap and freeze for up to 1 month. To release, turn the mold upside down. Place under running water until the ice releases.

1 Mix the rum, passion fruit pulp, the ½ cup of lime juice, the Cointreau, and the lime peel in a punch bowl and stir until the frozen passion fruit dissolves. Mix in the soda. Taste, adding more lime juice if desired.

2 Gently add the ice mold, top side facing up. Fill small cups with ice. Ladle punch into the glasses and garnish with the orchids, if desired.

TROPICOLADA

PUNCH

Banana, mango, pineapple, and coconut are featured in this variation of a piña colada. Cream of coconut can be found in the liquor department of most grocery stores. For a large party, make several batches up to one hour before guests arrive, and place them in the freezer to keep cold. Just before serving, pour the punch into a bowl and add an ice mold made with mango and pineapple (see Tips for Ice Molds, page 108). **SERVES 4**

4 cups ice cubes
1 ripe banana, peeled, cut into chunks
1½ cups chopped fresh or frozen mango
⅔ cup gold rum
½ cup pineapple juice
¼ cup canned sweetened cream of coconut
   (such as Coco López)
2 tablespoons fresh lime juice
2 tablespoons whipping cream
4 fresh mango wedges with skin (optional, for
   garnish)

1 Combine the ice cubes, banana, mango, rum, pineapple juice, cream of coconut, lime juice, and cream in a blender. Pulse the blender until the puree is smooth.

2 Divide the punch among 4 glasses. Garnish with the fresh mango wedges, if desired.

HIBISCUS
PUNCH

Dried hibiscus blossoms, also known as Jamaica flowers, have a tart, somewhat earthy flavor. (You can purchase them at Latin American markets.) They are brewed into a popular *agua fresca* and used in Mexican cooking in both savory and sweet recipes. For a nonalcoholic version, replace the tequila, mescal, and Cointreau with 2¼ cups sparkling water. **SERVES 6 TO 8**

2 ounces dried hibiscus flowers
¼ cup sugar
1½ cups silver tequila made from 100% agave
¼ cup mescal (optional)
½ cup fresh lime juice
½ cup Cointreau, or more to taste
6 to 8 Orange Sugar–Rimmed Glasses (see below)
Ice cubes
6 to 8 lime slices

ORANGE SUGAR–RIMMED GLASSES

Use a fine-holed Microplane or other grater to remove the zest from 1 orange. Mix the zest with ⅓ cup sugar on a small plate, stirring to release the orange oils. Rub the fruit of an orange wedge around the glass rims to moisten lightly. Dip the rims in the orange sugar to coat.

1 Place the hibiscus flowers in a mesh strainer and rinse briefly under running water. Place the flowers, sugar, and 3 cups water in a large saucepan. Bring to a boil over high heat, stirring until the sugar dissolves. Cool. Strain the liquid into a pitcher; discard the flowers, and chill until cold.

2 Stir the tea, tequila, mescal, and juice in a pitcher. Add the Cointreau and taste; add more, if desired.

3 Fill the sugar-rimmed glasses with ice. Ladle the punch over the ice. Garnish each with a lime slice.

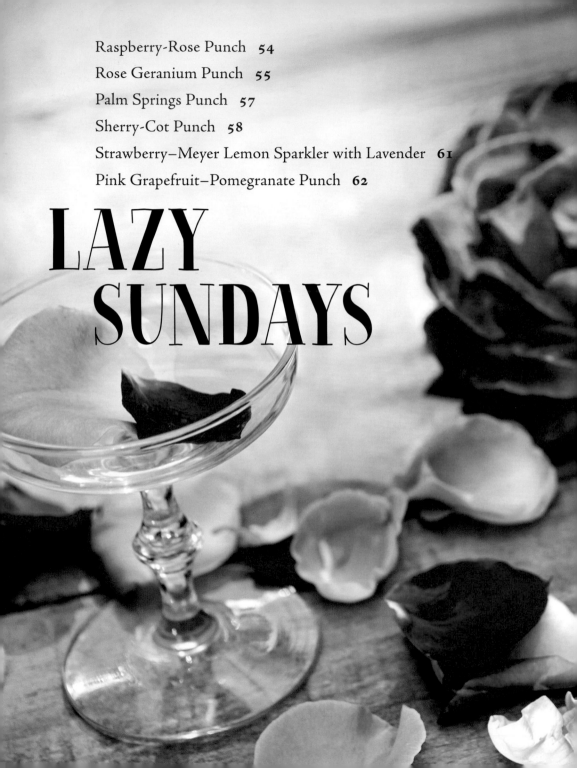

LAZY SUNDAYS

RASPBERRY-ROSE PUNCH (PAGE 54)

RASPBERRY-ROSE
PUNCH

Rose water is sold at some groceries, specialty foods stores, and Middle Eastern markets. The light musky flavor of the rose water will be cut right through by the fresh lime juice and sweet green tea. **SERVES 8**

2 6-ounce baskets fresh raspberries
(or 12 ounces frozen, thawed)
½ cup sugar
2 cups brewed green tea, chilled
⅔ cup fresh lime juice
½ to 1 cup gin, to taste
¼ teaspoon rose water
1½ cups chilled sparkling water
1 Raspberry Ice Mold (see below)
Unsprayed red and pink rose petals (optional, for garnish)
Ice cubes

RASPBERRY ICE MOLD

Fill a small mold with water to 2 inches from the top. Add 4 to 6 ounces raspberries (the berries will float). Freeze overnight or wrap the frozen mold tightly in plastic wrap and freeze for up to 1 month. To release, turn the mold upside down and place the bowl under running water until the ice releases.

1 Thoroughly mash the berries and sugar in a small bowl. Let stand for 30 minutes.

2 Strain the berries through a sieve set over a large bowl, pressing firmly on the fruit with a rubber spatula. Discard the seeds and mix the tea, lime juice, ½ cup gin, and rose water into the strained berry puree. Stir in the sparkling water and taste, adding up to ½ cup more gin if a stronger flavor is desired. Gently place the ice mold in a punch bowl, with the top side facing up. Pour the punch over the mold. Scatter rose petals over the punch, if desired.

3 Fill 8 cups with ice, and ladle the punch over the ice.

ROSE GERANIUM
PUNCH

This tart and floral drink features a simple syrup made with fragrant rose geranium leaves. You can find the plants at nursery stores and some farmer's markets.

SERVES 4

¾ cup Rose Geranium Simple Syrup (page 107)
¾ cup silver tequila made with 100% agave
⅓ cup fresh lime juice, or more to taste
¾ cup chilled sparkling water
Ice cubes
4 well-rinsed rose geranium leaves (optional, for garnish)
4 lime wedges (optional, for garnish)

1 Mix the syrup, tequila, and the ⅓ cup of lime juice in a large glass measuring cup. Mix in the sparkling water. Taste, adding more lime juice if desired.

2 Fill 4 small glasses with ice. Pour the punch over the ice. Tuck a rose geranium leaf into each glass and garnish with a lime wedge, if desired, and serve.

PALM SPRINGS
PUNCH

Vary the flavor of this drink using your favorite robustly flavored black tea, such as Earl Grey or English Breakfast. This is the type of punch you can make in a large batch to enjoy throughout the weekend. **SERVES 12**

5 strongly flavored tea bags, such as Earl Grey
1½ cups sugar
2¼ cups fresh lemon juice
2¼ cups vodka
2 lemons, sliced into rounds, seeds removed, plus
　　additional slices for garnish
Ice cubes

1 Bring 8 cups water to a boil in a large saucepan. Add the tea bags and remove the saucepan from the heat. Let the tea cool completely, then discard the tea bags. Mix the sugar into the tea; stir to dissolve. Mix in the lemon juice and vodka.

2 Pour the punch into a large pitcher or beverage container with a spigot; add the lemon slices. Refrigerate until cold, at least 2 hours and up to 8 hours.

3 Remove the punch from the refrigerator and add the ice. Fill 12 glasses with punch, garnish with additional lemon slices, and serve.

SHERRY-COT

PUNCH

A lovely combination of sherry and apricot (hence the portmanteau name), this would be a lovely addition to an afternoon tea—the perfect pairing to cucumber sandwiches, scones with whipped cream, and mini tartlets. **SERVES 8**

2 cups chilled apricot nectar
2 cups medium-dry sherry (such as Dry Sack)
6 tablespoons apricot or peach liqueur
3 tablespoons Amaretto liqueur
Pinch of ground cardamom
8 Flower Ice Cubes (see below) or regular ice cubes

FLOWER ICE CUBES

Place 1 nonpoisonous flower (such as lavender or pansy) in each empty square of an ice cube tray. Add water to cover the flowers and freeze overnight.

1 Combine the apricot nectar, sherry, apricot liqueur, Amaretto, and cardamom in a pitcher and stir to combine. Refrigerate for 1 hour.

2 Place an ice cube in each of 8 sherry glasses. Pour the punch over the ice and serve.

STRAWBERRY–MEYER LEMON
SPARKLER *with lavender*

Meyer lemons, noted for their unique fragrance, are thought to be a cross between a lemon and a mandarin orange. With lavender and fresh strawberries, this is a lovely afternoon drink. **SERVES 4**

12 large ripe strawberries, hulled
4 2-inch-long Meyer lemon peel strips
⅔ cup fresh Meyer lemon juice
½ cup vodka
½ cup Lavender Simple Syrup (page 107)
1 cup chilled sparkling water
Ice cubes
Fresh lavender sprigs (optional, for garnish)

1 Using a muddler or the handle of a wooden spoon, muddle the strawberries and lemon peels in a medium bowl. Pour in the lemon juice, vodka, and lavender syrup. Refrigerate for 1 hour to allow the flavors to develop.

2 Mix the sparkling water into the punch. Fill 4 glasses with ice. Ladle the punch mixture over the ice. Garnish with fresh lavender sprigs, if desired.

PINK GRAPEFRUIT–POMEGRANATE

PUNCH

These flavors are decadent—the floral St-Germain, the slightly bitter but juicy Campari—that you'll forget how good pink grapefruit and pomegranate are for you.

SERVES 12 TO 16

4 cups chilled fresh pink grapefruit juice

2 cups vodka

1 cup chilled 100% pomegranate juice (such as Pom)

½ cup St-Germain elderflower liqueur

⅓ cup Campari

2 cups chilled brut champagne or sparkling wine

1 Grapefruit-Pomegranate Ice Mold (see below)

Ice cubes

GRAPEFRUIT-POMEGRANATE ICE MOLD

Fill a mold with water to 2 inches from the top. Add slices of pink grapefruit, whole sections of pomegranate with the seeds still attached, and nonpoisonous leaves from citrus trees (the fruit and leaves will float). Freeze overnight; the frozen mold will keep for up to 2 weeks if wrapped in plastic. To release, turn the mold upside down under running water.

1 Mix the pink grapefruit juice, vodka, pomegranate juice, St-Germain, and Campari in a large punch bowl. Stir in the champagne.

2 Gently lower the ice mold into a large punch bowl, top side facing up. Fill the punch cups with ice. Ladle the punch over the ice into the cups.

HEIGHT OF SUMMER

SPIKED PINEAPPLE AGUA FRESCA
WITH SAGE AND SERRANO (PAGE 66)

SPIKED PINEAPPLE
AQUA FRESCA
with sage and serrano

Serrano chile livens up this fruity punch. The success of this drink depends on the fruit, so be sure to use only the ripest, most fragrant pineapple. **SERVES 4**

3 cups peeled and diced pineapple
¾ cup silver tequila made with 100% agave
¼ cup fresh lime juice
¼ cup sugar
8 sage leaves
1 serrano chile, halved and seeded
Ice cubes
Chilled sparkling water, for finishing the punch

1 Puree the pineapple and 2 cups water in a blender. Strain the puree through a sieve set over a bowl, pressing on the fruit to release its liquid.

2 Pour the puree into a large pitcher. Mix in the tequila, lime juice, and sugar. Bruise the sage leaves between your fingers and mix them into the punch. Add the serrano and stir for 30 seconds. Taste for spice level; leave the serrano to soak longer, or remove it if you like.

3 Fill 4 small glasses with ice. Pour in the punch and top with a splash of sparkling water.

THREE-MINUTE VODKA-LIME

PUNCH

This drink comes together in no time, with ingredients that can be kept in your freezer and pantry for any last-minute get-together. Look for Minute Maid limeade, as it has the brightest flavor (some generic ones have a bitter aftertaste). **SERVES 8**

1 cup vodka
½ cup frozen limeade concentrate
8 lime slices (from about 2 limes), seeds removed
2 cups chilled sparkling water
Ice cubes

1 Stir the vodka, limeade, and lime slices in a small pitcher until the limeade dissolves. Mix in the sparkling water.

2 Fill 8 short glasses with ice. Pour the punch over the ice and serve.

PEAR-BASIL
COOLER

A light and refreshing drink with a deep pear flavor, this is great in the late summer with just-harvested pears and basil. Later in the fall, try swapping rosemary for the basil. **SERVES 8**

8 large fresh basil leaves plus 8 fresh basil sprigs,
  for garnish
3 tablespoons fresh lemon juice
2 cups chilled pear nectar
¾ cup vodka
6 tablespoons pear vodka
6 tablespoons pear liqueur
2 cups chilled sparkling water
Ice cubes
8 thin pear slices, for garnish

1 Combine the basil leaves and lemon juice in a large pitcher. Using a muddler or the handle of a wooden spoon, press on the basil several times. Mix in the pear nectar, vodka, pear vodka, and pear liqueur. Let stand for 10 minutes. Remove the basil if desired. Add the sparkling water to the pear punch.

2 Fill 8 small stemmed or wine glasses with ice. Pour punch over the ice. Garnish each drink with a pear slice and a sprig of fresh basil.

WATERMELON–TEQUILA

PUNCH

After scooping out the watermelon, turn the empty shell into a punch bowl. Be sure to make this in summer when watermelon is in season and at its sweetest. Don't skip the chile salt rim on the glasses, as it balances the drink perfectly. **SERVES 6 TO 8**

1 large ripe seedless watermelon
¾ cup silver tequila made from 100% agave
½ cup fresh lime juice
¼ cup sugar
3 lime slices, seeds removed, plus 6 to 8 lime wedges
6 to 8 Chile Salt–Rimmed Glasses (see below)

CHILE SALT–RIMMED GLASSES

Mix 1 tablespoon kosher salt and ¾ teaspoon ground ancho or New Mexico chile on a plate. Run a lime wedge around the rim of each glass. Dip the glasses in the chile salt.

1 Cut off the top third of the long side of the watermelon. Cut a small slice off the rind of the opposite side so it can stand upright. Scoop out the flesh into a large bowl; refrigerate the watermelon "bowl" until ready to serve.

2 Working in batches, puree the watermelon in a blender. Strain the pureed watermelon through a sieve set over a large bowl. Mix 5 cups of the watermelon juice with the tequila, lime juice, and sugar in a large pitcher. Refrigerate until cold, about 1 hour.

3 Pour the punch into the watermelon bowl. Float lime slices on top. Fill rimmed glasses with ice. Ladle punch over the ice, and garnish with lime wedges.

SPIKED SPA
WATER

Spa water is the refreshing cucumber-, lemon-, and mint-infused water served at health clubs and hair salons. Here we've spiked it with vodka, imbuing the beverage with another level of healing. **SERVES 8**

2 English hothouse (seedless) cucumbers
6 thin lemon slices
20 fresh mint leaves
⅓ cup sugar
1 cup vodka
1 cup fresh lemon juice
2 cups chilled sparkling water
Ice cubes

1 Cut 12 slices from 1 cucumber; set aside. Peel the remaining cucumber and cut into small pieces; place in a blender with ½ cup water. Puree until smooth.

2 Using a muddler or the handle of a wooden spoon, muddle the sliced cucumber, lemon slices, mint leaves, and sugar in a medium bowl. Mix in 1¾ cups of the cucumber puree, the vodka, and the lemon juice. Cover and refrigerate for at least 2 and up to 8 hours to allow the flavors to develop.

3 Mix the sparkling water into the punch. Transfer the punch to a large pitcher.

4 Fill 8 glasses with ice. Pour the punch over the ice, allowing some sliced cucumber, lemon, and mint into each glass.

PEACHY
MOONSHINE

Also known as white lightning, moonshine is a high-proof distilled spirit. This version is tamed with peach nectar for a summer heat quencher. If you can't find moonshine, you can make the drink with ½ cup vodka, ¼ cup bourbon, and ¼ cup grappa. **SERVES 4**

3 cups chilled peach nectar
1 cup moonshine
⅔ cup fresh lemon juice
2 tablespoons Amaretto liqueur
Ice cubes
2 ripe medium peaches, sliced
　　(optional, for garnish)

1 Mix the peach nectar, moonshine, lemon juice, and Amaretto in a small pitcher.

2 Fill 4 small mason jars or glasses with ice and sliced peaches, if desired. Pour the punch over the ice and serve.

FIRESIDE COCKTAILS

BOOZY EGGNOG (PAGE 78)

BOOZY
EGGNOG

This eggnog gets its foamy texture from beaten egg whites. It can also be made without the egg whites and simply served as is over ice. **SERVES 6**

2 cups whipping cream

1 cup whole or low-fat milk

6 eggs, separated

½ cup plus 2 tablespoons sugar

1½ teaspoons pure vanilla extract

¼ cup gold rum

¼ cup brandy

¼ cup bourbon whiskey

Freshly grated nutmeg, for garnish

NOTE

This recipe contains raw egg whites and should not be served to pregnant women, the elderly, or anyone with a compromised immune system.

1 Bring the cream and milk to a simmer in a large heavy saucepan.

2 Whisk the egg yolks and ½ cup sugar in a large bowl until very light. Gradually whisk in the hot cream mixture (slowly, so the eggs don't cook). Return the mixture to the saucepan. Stir over medium-low heat until it thickens enough to coat the back of a spoon, about 8 minutes. Strain the liquid through a fine-mesh sieve into a bowl; mix in the vanilla. Chill uncovered until cold, then cover and keep refrigerated.

3 Mix the rum, brandy, and bourbon into the eggnog. Beat 3 egg whites with 2 tablespoons sugar in a bowl until soft peaks form (discard the remaining whites). Fold the beaten egg whites into the eggnog. Ladle the eggnog into cups, garnish with nutmeg, and serve.

SPICED PEAR
PUNCH

Pear replaces apple in this take on a winter favorite. This punch is ideal for sipping in front of the fire at a holiday party. **SERVES 10**

8 cups pear juice or pear nectar

4 cinnamon sticks, broken in half

24 whole cloves

1 cup pear vodka

10 thin lemon slices (from 1 or 2 lemons), seeds removed

10 thin pear slices

1 Bring the pear juice, cinnamon sticks, and cloves to boil in a heavy medium pot. Reduce the heat and simmer the liquid for 2 minutes.

2 Mix in the pear vodka, then the lemon and pear slices. Ladle the pear punch into 10 heat-proof mugs.

WINTER-SPICED RUM

PUNCH

Persimmons macerate in spiced rum for a unique fall punch. Star anise is added just five minutes before serving, as its flavor intensifies quickly. **SERVES 12**

8 cups white cranberry juice

3 cups spiced rum

¾ cup fresh lemon juice

¾ cup Allspice Simple Syrup (page 107)

2 Fuyu persimmons, stemmed, each cut into 4 slices

1 star anise

Ice cubes

1 Mix the cranberry juice, rum, lemon juice, allspice syrup, and persimmon slices in a large glass jar or pitcher. Refrigerate for at least 2 hours and up to 6 hours to allow the flavors to develop. Add the star anise and let it infuse for 5 minutes. Taste; remove the star anise if the flavor is pronounced, or allow to infuse for 5 more minutes.

2 Fill 12 small glasses with ice. Pour the punch over the ice and serve.

SWEDISH
GLÖGG

Mulled wine releases an intoxicating scent as it simmers, due to the array of spices and citrus. It's a great cold-weather drink, especially for a holiday party, so this recipe makes enough for a large crowd. **SERVES 16**

2 750-ml bottles dry red wine

2 cups ruby port

1 cup aquavit

½ cup sugar

1 cup blanched almonds

⅔ cup dried tart cherries

8 dried figs, quartered

6 orange peel strips

6 lemon peel strips

24 cardamom pods, slightly cracked with a mallet or rolling pin

1 teaspoon whole allspice

1 teaspoon whole black peppercorns

POMANDER BALL

Make a pomander ball to garnish the punch: Simply stud a whole orange with whole cloves in any pattern and add it to the glögg just before serving.

1 Combine all the ingredients in a large pot and bring to a simmer. Continue simmering over very low heat for 15 minutes, to allow the spice flavor to develop.

2 Transfer to a metal or porcelain punch bowl, if desired (or serve directly from the pot). Ladle the glögg into punch cups or mugs.

PUMPKIN
PATCH

Pumpkin ale and spiced rum are flavored with spices such as cinnamon, cloves, and allspice, in this great fall or winter drink. Look for pumpkin ale at liquor stores and upscale supermarkets, especially from October through February. SERVES 6

4 cups chilled pumpkin ale
½ cup spiced rum
4 teaspoons pure maple syrup
Ice cubes
1 whole nutmeg, for grating
6 cinnamon sticks, for garnish

1 Mix the ale, rum, and maple syrup in a small pitcher.

2 Fill 6 short glasses with ice. Pour the ale mixture over. Grate a little nutmeg over each glass, and garnish with a cinnamon stick.

CRANBERRY– GINGER

PUNCH

Not a gin drinker? This can be made with vodka instead. For a holiday party, make an ice mold with fresh limes and cranberries (see below) and serve the drink in a punch bowl. Be sure to start the ice mold at least one day ahead so it freezes solid. **SERVES 8**

1¼ cups gin
1 12-ounce can frozen cranberry juice cocktail
   concentrate
⅔ cup fresh lime juice
2 teaspoons grated peeled fresh ginger
3 cups chilled sparkling water
Cranberry-Lime Ice Mold (see below)
Ice cubes (optional)

CRANBERRY-LIME ICE MOLD

Add water to a mold, leaving about 2 inches at the top. Add cranberries, whole limes, lime slices, and lime leaves; the fruit will float. Freeze overnight or wrap the frozen mold tightly in plastic wrap and freeze for up to 1 month. To release, turn the mold upside down under running water.

1 Mix the gin, cranberry juice concentrate, lime juice, and ginger in a pitcher, stirring to dissolve the concentrate. Mix in the sparkling water.

2 Gently place the ice mold top side up in a punch bowl. Pour the punch over the ice mold. Ladle the punch into 8 glasses. Serve with ice if desired.

CAFÉ BRÛLOT

Spice, liqueur, and aromatics blend in this knock-out coffee drink. The original recipe for Café Brûlot was created at Antoine's restaurant in New Orleans in the 1890s and it's still served there, ignited tableside for a stunning presentation. **SERVES 8**

½ cup chilled whipping cream
1 tablespoon plus ¾ cup Grand Marnier
2 teaspoons plus ¼ cup packed brown sugar
1 teaspoon grated orange peel
12 ½ × 2-inch orange peel strips
8 ½ × 2-inch lemon peel strips
1 bay leaf
2 cinnamon sticks, broken in half
24 whole cloves
½ cup brandy
4 cups very strong freshly brewed coffee

1 Whisk the cream, 1 tablespoon of the Grand Marnier, 2 teaspoons of the brown sugar, and the grated orange peel in a medium bowl until it forms soft peaks. Cover and refrigerate the whipped cream until ready to serve.

2 Combine the remaining ¾ cup Grand Marnier, the remaining ¼ cup brown sugar, the citrus peel strips, bay leaf, cinnamon sticks, and cloves in a heavy medium saucepan or chafing dish. Stir over medium-low heat until the mixture begins to simmer. Simmer for 2 minutes, occasionally pressing on the citrus peels with a wooden spoon. Remove the liquid from the heat and let stand for 10 minutes to enhance the flavors.

3 Return the liquid to a simmer. (If desired, take it to the table in its saucepan at this time.) Add the brandy and carefully ignite with a long match (the flames will be high). Gradually add the coffee, causing the flames to subside. Ladle the liquid into 8 heat-proof mugs, leaving the citrus peels and spices behind in the saucepan. Top with the whipped cream.

CHAI MILK
PUNCH

Milk punch, a blend of milk and brandy or bourbon, dates back to the 1600s. Our version adds another traditional punch mixer, tea, as well as exotic spices. Rum lends a caramel smoothness, but brandy and bourbon would be good, too. Any variation is delicious served hot or over ice. **SERVES 6 TO 8**

20 whole cloves

15 cardamom pods

4 cinnamon sticks, broken in half, plus more whole sticks (optional, for garnish)

2 teaspoons whole black peppercorns

1 2-inch-long piece of peeled fresh ginger, sliced

5 black tea bags

2 cups whole milk

¼ cup packed brown sugar

½ cup gold rum (or brandy or bourbon)

1 Place the spices and ginger in a saucepan over medium heat. Using a muddler or a wooden spoon, crack the spices into pieces and bruise the ginger. Heat the spice mixture until lightly toasted, about 1 minute. Add 4 cups water and bring to a boil. Add the tea bags; remove from the heat and let steep for 5 minutes. Discard the tea bags, and add the milk and brown sugar. Cover and let stand for 5 minutes.

2 Return the chai to a simmer. Mix in the rum. Ladle into heat-proof cups, leaving the spices behind. Garnish each cup with a cinnamon stick, if desired.

AZTEC CHOCOLATE

PUNCH

Tequila and brandy lend the punch to this after-dinner drink, an easy stand-in for dessert. Serve it hot in the winter, or chilled over ice in the summer. For a non-alcoholic version, simply omit the brandy and tequila.

SERVES 6

1 cup chilled whipping cream
2 tablespoons packed dark brown sugar, plus more
   if desired
4 tablespoons brandy
4 cups whole or low-fat milk
1 cup (6 ounces) bittersweet chocolate chips
2 cinnamon sticks, broken in half
1 tablespoon unsweetened cocoa powder
¾ teaspoon ground ancho chile, plus more for garnish
¼ teaspoon freshly grated nutmeg
¼ teaspoon ground allspice
Pinch of salt
⅓ cup tequila or mescal

1 Whisk the cream, 2 tablespoons of the brown sugar, and 2 tablespoons of the brandy in a large bowl until softly whipped. Chill the whipped cream until ready to use.

2 Bring the milk, chocolate chips, cinnamon sticks, cocoa powder, the ¾ teaspoon of ground chile, the

nutmeg, allspice, and salt to a simmer in a heavy medium saucepan over medium heat, whisking frequently. Simmer for 2 minutes. Discard the cinnamon sticks. Add the tequila and the remaining 2 tablespoons brandy. Taste, adding up to 1 tablespoon of brown sugar if a sweeter flavor is desired.

3 Ladle the punch into heat-proof mugs or cups. Top with the whipped cream and sprinkle with additional ground chile.

NONALCOHOLIC PUNCHES

MIXED BERRY LEMONADE (PAGE 94)

MIXED BERRY
LEMONADE

Although ideal in spring or summer, this can be made year-round: It uses frozen berries, which are often juicier and more flavorful than fresh. **SERVES 6**

⅔ cup frozen unsweetened mixed berries
    (blackberries, raspberries, blueberries), thawed
½ cup sugar
½ cup fresh lemon juice
1 tablespoon grated lemon peel
2 cups chilled sparkling water, or more to taste
Ice cubes

1 Combine the berries, sugar, lemon juice, lemon peel, and ¼ cup water in a large jar or pitcher. Stir until the sugar dissolves. Chill until cold, about 1 hour. Gently stir in 2 cups of the sparkling water; taste, and add more sparkling water if desired.

2 Fill 6 glasses with ice. Pour the punch into the glasses and serve.

ISLAND GIRL

PUNCH

This nonalcoholic tropical juice blend isn't too sweet, making it great for a baby shower or birthday party where adults and kids share the same refreshment.

SERVES 12

4 cups chilled guava nectar
2 cups chilled coconut water
2 cups chilled fresh pink grapefruit juice
2 cup chilled sparkling water
1 cup chilled pineapple juice
1 small banana, peeled and sliced
2 guavas, sliced (optional)
Ice cubes

Mix everything but the ice in a large pitcher or a drink dispenser with a spigot. Add the ice to fill the pitcher, and pour into 12 glasses.

FIFTY-FIFTY
PUNCH

This classic kids' punch tastes just like a Creamsicle or 50-50 bar, the ice-cream-truck fave. For an adults-only version, add a splash of Grand Marnier and/or a drop of orange-flower water, if desired. **SERVES 4**

1 cup frozen orange juice concentrate
2 ¼-inch-thick orange slices, each cut in half
3 teaspoons finely grated orange peel
2 cups chilled sparkling water
Ice cubes
1 pint premium vanilla ice cream

1 Stir the orange juice concentrate, orange slices, and 2 teaspoons of the grated orange peel in a small pitcher until the concentrate thaws. Mix in the sparkling water.

2 Fill 4 tall glasses with ice. Pour the punch over the ice, and top each glass with a scoop of vanilla ice cream. Sprinkle with the remaining 1 teaspoon of orange peel. Serve immediately with long spoons and straws.

SPARKLING PEACH BLOSSOM
PUNCH

Enjoy this sparkler on a hot summer afternoon or served alongside a boozy party punch as a festive nonalcoholic alternative. **SERVES 10**

1 Peach Ice Mold (see below)
3 cups white cranberry–peach juice cocktail
2⅔ cups chilled peach nectar
1⅓ cups chilled sparkling water
1⅓ cups freshly brewed green tea, chilled
¼ cup fresh lemon juice
2 large ripe peaches, sliced (optional, for garnish)
Ice cubes

PEACH ICE MOLD

Add water to a mold, leaving about 2 inches at the top. Add peach slices, lemon slices, and some lemon leaves if available, arranging them in a decorative fashion (the ingredients will float). Freeze overnight or wrap the frozen mold tightly and freeze for up to 1 month. To release, turn the mold upside down. Place under running water until the ice releases.

1 Place the ice mold, top side facing up, in a large punch bowl. Add the cranberry-peach juice cocktail, peach nectar, sparkling water, tea, and lemon juice to the bowl, and stir to combine. Add the peach slices to garnish, if using.

2 Fill 10 punch cups or wine glasses with ice. Ladle the punch and some of the fruit, if using, over the ice and serve.

VAMPIRE
BREW

Dry ice adds a spooky, foggy touch to this Halloween punch. In addition to the general safety tips below, check out dryiceinfo.com for important information about working with dry ice. **SERVES 16 TO 20**

3 quarts cherry juice
4 12-ounce bottles Coca-Cola
Food-grade dry ice (see below)

SAFETY TIPS FOR DRY ICE

+ *Store the dry ice in an insulated cooler (never in the fridge or freezer).*

+ *Do not allow dry ice to come in contact with bare skin.*

+ *Use tongs or gloves when handling dry ice.*

+ *Use only a metal punch bowl, as a glass one will shatter.*

+ *Do not combine regular ice with dry ice.*

+ *Use dry ice only in well-ventilated areas.*

+ *Have an adult ladle the punch into cups to be sure no pieces of ice end up in individual servings.*

+ *Never allow children to handle dry ice.*

1 Mix the cherry juice and cola in a metal punch bowl. Using tongs or gloves, place 1 large piece of dry ice directly into the punch; the mixture will bubble vigorously and create a fog. (Alternatively, you can place a metal bowl of water behind the punch bowl and add dry ice to the water, so the fog will appear as a background effect only. In that scenario, add regular ice to the punch to chill.)

2 Ladle the punch into cups.

PEPPERMINT STICK ICE CREAM
PUNCH

Kids will love this delicious holiday treat with its edible candy cane stirring stick. For an adult version, add a splash of vodka. **SERVES 4**

1½ pints premium peppermint stick ice cream
2 cups chilled sparkling water
Ice cubes
4 large candy canes, for garnish
Crushed candy canes (optional)

1 Mix ½ cup of the ice cream with the sparkling water in a large glass measuring cup, stirring until the ice cream melts.

2 Fill 4 tall glasses with ice. Pour the soda mixture over the ice. Top each glass with a scoop of ice cream. Garnish each glass with a candy cane and sprinkle with crushed candy canes, if desired. Serve immediately with long spoons and straws.

WASSAIL

Wassail is a hot mulled apple cider punch that was created in southern England, where, in ancient times, it was part of a winter ritual to ensure a good apple harvest the following year. Nowadays it's sipped because it's tasty—and you can add a splash of brandy, bourbon, or rum for a grown-up kick. **SERVES 4**

1 quart apple cider

4 2-inch-long orange peel strips

2 tablespoons honey

1 tablespoon fresh lemon juice

10 whole cloves

10 whole allspice

10 whole green cardamom pods, crushed

3 cinnamon sticks, each broken in half; plus
    4 whole cinnamon sticks (optional, for garnish)

4 crab apples, a slit cut in the bottom of each
    (optional, for garnish)

1 Combine the cider, orange peel strips, honey, lemon juice, cloves, allspice, cardamom pods, and cinnamon sticks in a heavy medium saucepan, and bring to a boil. Reduce the heat and simmer for 5 minutes to infuse the spice flavors.

2 Ladle the cider into 4 heat-proof mugs. Garnish each mug with a crab apple wedged onto the rim and a whole cinnamon stick, if desired.

FLAVORED SYRUPS

Simple syrup is a mix of water and sugar that is integral at any bar as a quick way to add sweetness to cocktails. The syrup can be steeped with a variety of flavors including herbs, flowers, citrus, and spice. The syrups will keep for several weeks in the refrigerator.

BASIC SIMPLE SYRUP

MAKES ABOUT 1 CUP

¾ cup sugar
¾ cup water

Stir the sugar and water in a small saucepan over medium-low heat until the sugar dissolves. Increase the heat and bring the syrup to a boil. Immediately add the following ingredients depending on the variation being used.

FOR GINGER SIMPLE SYRUP: Add 1 tablespoon chopped peeled fresh ginger to the boiling syrup; cover, remove from the heat, and let stand until cool. Strain the syrup through a fine-mesh sieve into a jar. Seal the jar and refrigerate.

FOR LEMON VERBENA SIMPLE SYRUP: Stir ¼ cup lemon verbena leaves into the boiling syrup; cover, remove from the heat, and let stand until cool. Strain the syrup through a fine-mesh sieve into a jar. Seal the jar and refrigerate.

FOR MINT SIMPLE SYRUP: Stir ¼ cup mint leaves into the boiling syrup; cover, remove from the heat, and let stand until cool. Strain the syrup through a fine-mesh sieve into a jar. Seal the jar and refrigerate.

FOR LAVENDER SIMPLE SYRUP:
Stir 2 teaspoons culinary lavender blossoms into the boiling syrup; remove from the heat, cover, and let stand until cool. Strain the syrup through a fine-mesh sieve into a jar. Seal the jar and refrigerate.

FOR ROSE GERANIUM SIMPLE SYRUP: Stir 1 cup rose geranium leaves into the boiling syrup; remove from the heat, cover, and let stand until cool. Strain the syrup through a fine mesh sieve and into a jar. Seal the jar and refrigerate.

FOR LIME SIMPLE SYRUP:
Stir the peel of 2 limes into the boiling syrup; remove from the heat, cover, and let stand until cool. Strain the syrup through a fine-mesh sieve and into a jar. Seal the jar and refrigerate.

FOR ALLSPICE SIMPLE SYRUP:
Stir 1 slightly rounded teaspoonful of whole allspice into the boiling syrup; reduce the heat and simmer for 30 seconds. Remove from the heat, cover, and cool. Strain the syrup through a fine-mesh sieve into a jar. Seal the jar and refrigerate.

FOR RHUBARB SIMPLE SYRUP:
Slice 2 stalks rhubarb into 1-inch chunks (about 2 cups). Stir the rhubarb into the boiling syrup; remove from the heat, cover, and let stand without stirring until cool. Strain the syrup into a jar. Seal the jar and refrigerate.

TIPS FOR ICE MOLDS

- Punch bowls vary considerably in size. Before making an ice mold, measure the width of your punch bowl. Choose a mold that is at least 3 inches smaller than the width of the punch bowl so it will easily fit inside. (Don't have a punch bowl? Try using a soup tureen, decorative bowl, or trifle dish.) If you don't have a plastic or silicone mold made for the purpose, try a Bundt pan, ring mold, soufflé dish, or bowl.

- If using flowers in your ice mold or ice cubes, be sure to use unsprayed, nonpoisonous ones, such as roses, dendrobium orchids, pansies, carnations, hibiscus, lavender, and marigolds. If you're not sure about the flowers you're selecting, ask your local florist what's safe to use in food.

- Make the ice mold at least 1 day ahead so the ice freezes solid. The ice mold will last in the freezer for about 1 month; just leave it in its container and cover it with foil to help prevent freezer burn.

PUNCHES BY TYPE OF ALCOHOL

This list is a quick shortcut if you're looking to clean out your liquor cabinet with one of these delicious punches. Some of these recipes incorporate additional bitters or more specialty liqueurs, such as crème de cacao, limoncello, or Amaretto, so check each recipe for the full list of ingredients before you start preparing your drink.

GIN-BASED

Pimm's Punch (**page 10**)

Jungle Juice (**page 16**)

Gin Fizz with Lemon Verbena (**page 23**)

Raspberry-Rose Punch (**page 54**)

Cranberry-Ginger Punch (**page 85**)

VODKA-BASED

Skinny Moscow Mule (**page 15**)

Jungle Juice (**page 16**)

Bloody Mary Punch with Fennel (**page 19**)

Meyer Lemon Drop Champagne Punch (**page 34**)

Palm Springs Punch (**page 57**)

Strawberry–Meyer Lemon Sparkler with Lavender (**page 61**)

Pink Grapefruit–Pomegranate Punch (**page 62**)

Three-Minute Vodka-Lime Punch (**page 67**)

Pear-Basil Cooler (**page 69**)

Spiked Spa Water (**page 73**)

Spiced Pear Punch (**page 79**)

WHISKEY- OR BOURBON-BASED

Julep-Tea Punch (**page 11**)

Old Fashioned–Manhattan Punch (**page 12**)

Iced Irish Coffee Stout Punch (**page 20**)

Peachy Moonshine (**page 74**)

Boozy Eggnog (**page 78**)

RUM-BASED

Jungle Juice (**page 16**)

White Sangria Exotique (**page 29**)

Planter's Punch (**page 41**)

Mai Tai Punch (**page 42**)

Lychee Mojito Punch (**page 45**)

Passion Fruit Punch (**page 46**)

Tropicolada Punch (**page 49**)

Boozy Eggnog (**page 78**)

Winter-Spiced Rum Punch (**page 81**)

INDEX